Orpheus on the Beach
and an Orange Chair

Orpheus on the Beach and an Orange Chair

A collection of poems by Laraine Kentridge Lasdon

For my late husband Leon and my daughter
Claire always there in spirit and space

Contents

Orpheus on the Beach
and an Orange Chair

Audition

I look out from the front of the stage
afraid to be found. A disembodied voice
wraps around me asking cold hard facts
from the disaffected black of the theater.
A solitary beam of light probes my pale face.
Give me your name, date of birth,
Where are you from. Why are you here?

From an abyss of not knowing
I try desperately to speak.
Puffs of air spiral from dry lips, soundless,
yet in the next few crucial seconds
I am compelled to seek a self

Who am I, what am I? A churning of ideas.
Am I Ophelia tossing rosemary for remembrance,
drowned by indifferent love or angry Martha
bourbon-tippled with no thought of temperance,
destined to live forever in fevered disappointment.

Am I the delicate lilac, or a field
of wild grasses that sigh and wave?
Can I claim to be the "unravished rose" of Oscar Wilde
offering it's heady fragrance to the world?

Who am I, what am I?
Standing here, stripped, alone,
a desire for clarity takes hold.
An astonishing vigor fills my soul.

Who am I, where am I from beats in my heart.
Anyone, anywhere, you are not lost.
It's your choice, you have ten seconds,
says the voice.

From the front of the stage in the beam of light,
I choose the girl from the past, holding tight to the boy,
part innocent, part rebel, lost in a kiss, sitting on stairs,
leaning on a sign that says "Do not sit on the steps"

Cue lights!

My Jazz Heart

It's the heart,
that gives me trouble,
locked up for so long.
Afraid, unable to keep up
with 75 years. Raving, pulsing,
it's a noisy heart. As if I need
a signal at all times to feel
conjoined, able to touch.
Sometimes it is all too much

There is always a year,
a week or a day that does the
jangle jive. I can't get out of it,
find the quiet beat of my heart.

But, in the morning and at sunset
I slip into the swimming pool
and float on my back, hair spreading out,
black against blue. My pulse is a deep
base, soothing, an even rhythm,
cool jazz, the way I like it.

Flamenco Birds

My small balcony is occupied
by two chattering birds
clicking their clawed feet
on the railing, prancing,
synchronized, proud flamenco dancers.
Their black heads turn,
eyes lock, beaks clattering castanets.
My hand lightly touched the door handle.
At once, arched breast, wings strumming,
away! Unlike the pain of my loss that
like an albatross cannot fly.
They are gone, into the morning air.
The performance murmurs a last vibration.
¡Olé! I whisper. Sitting alone in my old blue chair.

The Troubadour's Song

The troubadour's voice soars out
through the rafters of the sun-filled hall,
hovers and shivers and falls
in the heat of the thermal vortex coiling.
as distant thunder becomes his percussion
signaling a storm to accompany deep emotion.

Centuries ago, troupes of jugglers, poets,
and ecstatics sang of Kings and Queens,
battles and dreams, and everyday things.
Proclaiming the news they roamed wild and free
as the people tumbled from huts, abandoned their fields,
sweating and shouting their curiosity.

I listen, entranced at the border of madness and joy,
in thrall to the truths of the poet-storyteller.
He stands on a stage, with challenge and invitation
plucks his guitar. The first single note.
Thus begins his tale of reflection. I listen, eyes closed.

He seems to sing to me. Know the stories of sad peoples,
unjust laws, and grandfathers who worked in glue factories
and fought world wars for us.
Guitar chords pierce through our placid acceptance,
each note pulling and plucking, seeking asylum in my consciousness,
every word pegged to the taut rope of music and prayer
sung out clearly, so there can be no mistake
of a Hallelujah and grace,
revelations and praise in each phrase.

A little miracle of space and sound to breathe.

The voice of the troubadour becomes throaty, a growl.
First low, then falsetto, gently flowing through me, lyrical yet grand.
Our hearts are the strings singing "I do understand"
I am the woman of the folk song.
I weep for the sad people,
I weep at unjust laws andI weep and
pledge to honor the generations of wars.

He ends his story with a quiet minor chord,
the chorus of our sigh.
A hymn.

Eyes bright with tears,
he cradles his guitar,
hitches up his jeans,
and moves on, wild and free,
to sing his song again.

Seductive Climates

The honeyed sun
warms my chilled skin,
not yet recovered from
a rogue blast. Bastard blizzard,
rending trees helpless, cracked,
bent over by the tumultuous
tears of ice of an angry winter.

I close my eyes, time to breathe
the seductive air of spring,
the perfume of the sun, aromatic ambergris,
redolent of swollen Molucca Island seas.

Sweet tobacco, sandalwood,
nutmeg, the forever spice
of your old tweed jacket,
rough on my cheek.
We danced as deities
the night we met.

Passions enlivened the delight
of our virginal lust,
words ended as sighs on our lips.
We hardly noticed the fading light.
He conversed about Le Corbusier:
The brute force of the concrete.
I quoted Baudelaire, prescient:
"oh dangerous woman,
O seductive climates!
Will I adore your snow and your frosts?"

I close my eyes.
Feel the chill on my skin.
Winter comes too soon, again.
Love cracks and bends as winter descends.
Ice tears sting. Soul-death burial, blue-white snow.
When Spring returns,
new sap flows.

Primavera Ghosted

where are you
where are you
are you where the roses fall
and curl in loamy soil

where are you
where are you
are you where the bird
flies in the open sky

where are you
gone are you
gone

The man who left his wife

The headline thrummed
with the news of moral decay
when a man could leave his wife,
divorce after a lifetime, a life
dedicated to doing good,
native to his personality
until he remembered, now,
the first funeral he went to
and how the thud of the soil
shocked him when, at the age of six,
he was cocky and exempt from fear
and felt only courage. He pulled away
from his mother and ran as no runner
had run before and cried and cried
as he hid behind the car.
He felt that fear now at 84
and left to go he did not know where,
it just had to be very, very far.

"I've been killing orchids forever."

Her black, marble headstone is covered with dusty dry grass. I balance on both knees, and with the corner of my coat, brush off the debris.

In each hand I hold a fistful of pebbles,
smooth, some jagged, like our relationship.
Each small rock will settle on the granite,
finding a nesting spot to rest.
I thought of words of gratitude and love we never said aloud.
But her words, a litany of what might have been,
should have been, seemed to be written in the fresher green grasses
nestling along the edges of her small tomb.

My mother's life had the destiny of an orchid. A single stem with eight blooms. Eight decades. Nothing in her past prepared her to cultivate and nurture either herself or her children. Consider her angry British father, working the railroads, an Inspector. He immigrated to a grim, small town, in South Africa, arriving with a frail spouse who succumbed to depression and an institution, rarely seeing her daughter. Both starving for affection.

The orchid blossoms' petals arc towards light.
In the shadows is a barely noticed wilting
tinged with melancholy, yearning
for the loyalty of a bright day.
For my mother, a flower from that stem died every decade.

As she lay dying in a small clinic in Cape Town, she whispered to me that she had been killing orchids forever. "I never found my sun"

I kneel, your ashes buried beneath me.
I place eight white pebbles on your headstone.
These will never die.

Orpheus on the Beach

It might as well be Orpheus,
dead on the island peninsula.
A grey silence, a grand conceit,
controlled the surly sea.
No restful lullabies,
a fling of sandpiper's wheet-wheet eighth notes
carried away by the wind.
Gulls sullen in the graffiti painted
tunnel where the only recognizable
image is on the entrance wall.
A single man paddling a skewed canoe,
on a green sea, a craft of blue

One foot in front of the other,
I made my way over tidal seaweed
towards a sculpted black rock,
carved by salt and foam,
a baroque nude
reclining on the shore,
pulsing to the rhythm
of ocean thunders.
In the curve of her ebony elbow
was an orange chair.
I sat.

My chair became a vessel,
strangely comforting, graceful,
slipping down and over
curved waves to the edge of time.
The sun began to sing,
to the music of the sea, the slap
of the wings of diving gulls,
their coarse calls a counterpoint to my melancholy.
An infinite symphony.

Thank you for appearing here, this year,
searching for your Eurydice.
The mystery and wonder
of my place in the world, clear.
My future is not my past, I see,
Oh, Orpheus, do not look back,
move forward, resolute,
in vision and melody.

My Sister Thee Tree

I fling myself into her skirts of green,
cling to her sticky veins of chlorophyl.
A sunshine halo on her sky-high branch,
shines in my eyes. I let her leaves, thick,
wet and tangy with summer, caress my skin.
My ears hear a chorus, senses alive,
glorious music of air, light, and life,

Today possibility and reality collide.
I blend and melt into my sister, my benign
symbiont nurturing and strong,
a perfect host to calm my erratic fear.
Seeking truth, growing towards my need,
my sister tree, even as a weed,
opens herself to me,
accepting my organic greed
to feed on the very essence of nature.

Gathering strength to journey
through drenching summer rains, nourishing
swirling roots and soil to searing drought.
Like the lovers we were, who parted,
forever, lips parched for lost kisses.
Wrapped in her green robes,
I can be cool, damp, hidden, and whole,
until the sun, its high-pitched heated song,
finds my refuge.

Now thee, sister, guardian tree,
faces winter with me. The last leaf drifting down.
I am curled on hard cold ground,
face pressed into her rough bark.
I find peace in her deep
maternal humming, the rustle of her roots.

Small joys persist as the last
of the hardy sparrows flit through
dry labyrinths of twigs and branch,
preparing to depart the freezing rain.
Oh my love – will we, like the winter tree
hold on until the next season, and the next.
Can the magic of possibility, reality, co-exist?

I am your tree. Hold onto me.
Suspended between love and loss.
No time to reap, plant and heal.

"In Memoriam"

I see your sadness
in the curve of your head
downward slope of a shoulder
an ocean swelling in your eyes

I see your sadness
so I offer a forest
of wild roses,
a cape of the softest
lambs wool embroidered
with chrysanthemums
and three plump doves
to hover above
a halo, a symbol
of your pure joy.

I see your sadness
in your stillness
I use magic
wizardry and incantations
and offer you seven
white cats, manifestations
of ghostly Hannah, sweetest cat
forever cuddled on your lap.

www.ingramcontent.com/pod-product-compliance
Lightning Source LLC
Chambersburg PA
CBHW060359130626
46553CB00003B/1304